IMAGES
of America

BOSTON
A CENTURY OF PROGRESS

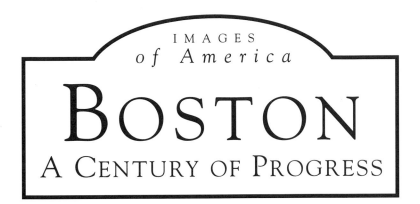

IMAGES
of America

BOSTON
A CENTURY OF PROGRESS

Anthony Mitchell Sammarco

ARCADIA

First published 1995
Copyright © Anthony Mitchell Sammarco, 1995

ISBN 0-7524-0253-6

Published by Arcadia Publishing,
an imprint of the Chalford Publishing Corporation
One Washington Center, Dover, New Hampshire 03820
Printed in Great Britain

Library of Congress Cataloging-in-Publication Data applied for

In *Over the Teacups*, Oliver Wendell Holmes said of the "telescope man" on the Boston Common: "Ever since I had a ten-cent look at the transit of Venus . . . through the telescope in the Mall, the earth has been wholly different to me from what it used to be."

Contents

Acknowledgments

In researching the history and development of Boston during the nineteenth century, I have been fascinated with the aspects of topographical and social transformations.

Boston: A Century of Progress is the compilation of a series of lectures presented before the Boston Public Library, the Boston Society of Architects, the Boston Center for Adult Education, the New England Chapter of the Victorian Society, and various other preservation groups. These lectures, which are enhanced by evocative and poignant visual images, allow one to see how dramatically Boston has changed.

I would like to thank the following people for their continued support and encouragement: Daniel Ahlin, Anthony Bognanno, John Burrows, Paul and Helen Buchanan, Ellen Clegg ("City Weekly," *The Boston Globe*), Lorna Condon (Society for the Preservation of New England Antiquities), Rupert Davis, Richard Fitzgerald (Boston Society of Architects), Rosamond Gifford, Edward Gordon (The Gibson House Museum), Pauline Chase Harrell, Harry Katz, James Z. Kyprianos, Robert J. MacMillan, M.D., Stephen D. Paine, Reverend Michael Parise, William H. Pear, Sally Pierce (Boston Athenaeum), Dennis Ryan, Anthony and Mary Mitchell Sammarco, Rosemary Sammarco, Sylvia Sandeen, Robert Bayard Severy, Catharina Slautterback (Boston Athenaeum), Joyce Stevens (Heritage Education), Sandra Storey (Gazette Publications), Kenneth Turino, William Varrell, Dorothy C. Wallace, William S. Young, and Arcadia's Kirsty Sutton and Jim Burkinshaw.

Royalties from this book will benefit the Sammarco Print Room Fund of The Boston Athenaeum.

Introduction

In a cast of votes, the citizens of Boston incorporated their ancient and historic town as the "City of Boston" on March 4, 1822. Faneuil Hall was the scene of celebration as the Charter of 1822 allowed for a mayor and a board of aldermen who would govern the new city. The charter stated that the mayor should be "vigilant and active at all times in causing the laws of the government . . . to be duly executed and put in force." Words to live by, but the sweeping changes that would take place in Boston during the ensuing century would certainly put the mayor and his aldermen to the test.

From fewer than 50,000 residents in 1822, Boston swelled both in population and land as the century progressed. To accommodate the increasing population and waves of immigrants from Europe, the original land mass of Boston was increased by cutting down hills and filling in marshlands. The western marshes, known as "Back Bay," would be filled in during the last five decades of the nineteenth century to create one of America's premier residential neighborhoods.

More than just topographical and social changes were taking place. As the "Athens of America," Boston led the country in educational reform, and the establishment of the Boston Public Library and its network of neighborhood branches reached out to residents. The industrialization and growth of business brought railroads to the area, which linked the city to the suburbs and beyond. These railroads were a marvel of their day, and had magnificent stations that reflected the importance of their achievement.

Boston continued to expand through new land and towns that were annexed to the city, including: Roxbury, Dorchester, Charlestown, Brighton, West Roxbury (including Jamaica Plain and Roslindale), and Hyde Park. As this expansion continued, the new residents joined forces with the Boston Brahmins in creating a thriving nexus of culture, business, and philanthropy in the nineteenth century.

Boston: A Century of Progress is the story of the city's growth from 1822 to 1922 in photographs. These images chronicle the tremendous changes that have taken place in Boston, so revel in the accomplishments of our ancestors and see the events that shaped Boston's destiny.

Sicut Patribus, Sit Deus Nobis!

One
The North End

The City of Boston Relief Station in Haymarket Square was designed by Sturgis and Brigham. It provided medical services to those in the North End and the West End. This photograph shows the kiosk of the Haymarket subway stop in the foreground with North Washington Street (leading to Causeway Street) on the right.

The Old North Church on Salem Street in Boston's North End was built in 1723. It is known by schoolchildren across America as the church whose steeple housed the lanterns that signaled to Paul Revere "one if by land, two if by sea," as immortalized in Longfellow's poem.

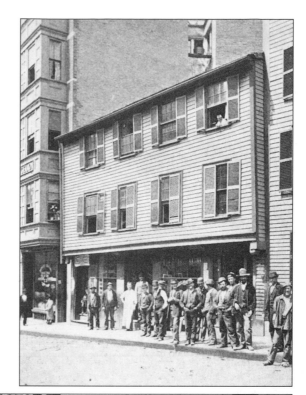

The Paul Revere House on North Square was home to the patriot from 1770 to 1800. In the late nineteenth century the house was used as the F.A. Goduti cigar factory and later as the Banca Italiana for the Italian community. Restored by Joseph Everett Chandler in 1907, it is now the oldest surviving house from the Colonial era.

Copp's Hill Burying Ground was laid out on Hull Street in the North End. On all sides of the cemetery were houses built closely together. In the rear, the Bunker Hill Monument in Charlestown rises above the neighborhood.

By the time of the Revolution the North End was a neighborhood of small houses. The Tileston House was built at the corner of Prince and Margaret Streets about 1670.

The North End had numerous "alleys" that wound their way from one street to another. One of these, Salutation Alley, still runs from Hanover Street to Commercial Street. When this photograph was taken in the 1890s Salutation Alley was a maze of tenements.

The Fitchburg Railroad Depot on Causeway Street was an impressive Gothic Revival train station designed by George Dexter in 1847. It connected Boston and Fitchburg via the "Hoosic Tunnel Route."

The Boston Stone was placed on Marshall Street in 1737, and since that time it has been the point from which all locations measure their distance from Boston.

The Prince Street Playground was laid out in 1913 and was separated from the street by a stucco pergola. The playground beautified the North End, which had very little open space, with grass and shrubs.

North Station on Causeway Street was designed by Shepley, Rutan, and Coolidge and built in 1893 to connect Boston with northern cities and towns. Seen in the foreground is the North Station stop on "the Elevated" (or "the El," as it was known).

Two
The Waterfront

The Commonwealth Dock Head House was built in 1912 for ocean liners docking in Boston. With its impressive arcaded facade, it projected into Boston Harbor to accommodate the massive liners. It is now the World Trade Center.

Faneuil Hall, given to the Town of Boston by Peter Faneuil, was built in 1742 as a market with a hall above. In 1805, Charles Bulfinch doubled the width of the building and added a third story for the Ancient and Honorable Artillery Company.

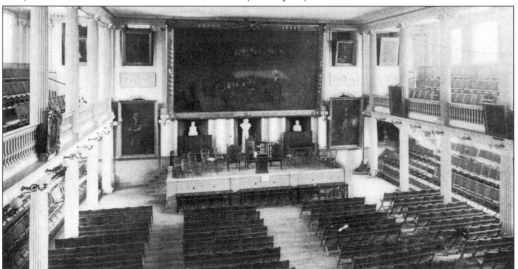

The interior of Faneuil Hall is as impressive as the exterior. Above the dais is a monumental painting of Daniel Webster debating before the State House. To the sides of the dais are portraits of Peter Faneuil (left) and President George Washington (right). It was in this hall on March 4, 1822, that Boston became a city.

Quincy Market, located just east of
Faneuil Hall, was named for Josiah
Quincy, the second mayor of Boston. It
was designed by Alexander Parris and
built between 1825 and 1826. When
this c. 1895 photograph was taken, the
market was flanked by the North (on
the right) and South Markets which
had counting rooms, offices, and
numerous restaurants, including
Cottrell's and the famous Durgin Park
Restaurant.

The old Boston Custom House was
designed by Charles Bulfinch and
served as the custom office until 1847.

The T Wharf extended from Long Wharf in the shape of a "T." The water surrounding the wharf was known as Portuguese Harbor, as numerous Portuguese had settled in Boston and New Bedford and worked there as fishermen. The small boats shown here were fishing boats.

Boston Harbor was extended by the addition of wharves on the east and north shores. Some of the wharves were small, but Long Wharf extended the furthest and was actually a continuation of State Street.

The new Boston Custom House was built on the edge of the waterfront by Ammi Burnham Young in 1847. It had impressive Doric columns that supported a dome.

The "telescope man" offered both children and adults a view of the heavens for 10¢. From his extension telescope on the Boston Common the curious could see the stars and planets or just interesting views of Boston.

South Station, located at the corner of Atlantic Avenue and Summer Street, was completed in 1899. Its rail services connected Boston and the South Shore cities and towns. At one point it also featured an elevated train (shown on the right) which ran above the traffic along Atlantic Avenue and connected South Station to North Station.

During the heyday of rail travel, the waiting room at South Station had coffered ceilings, tile floors, and distinctive bronze and glass booths where one could purchase newspapers, magazines, and candy. South Station has recently been restored and it is now the Amtrak terminal.

Strung along Atlantic Avenue were numerous buildings with retail space on the first floor and factory and production rooms above. This is a c. 1895 photograph of the Joseph P. Manning Company, located near Hanover Street. It sold pipes and tobaccos, and was the first commercial concern in Boston to adopt automobiles for delivery service.

The Hotel Essex was built opposite South Station at the corner of Essex Street and Atlantic Avenue. This eleven-story hotel was a great favorite with people traveling through South Station.

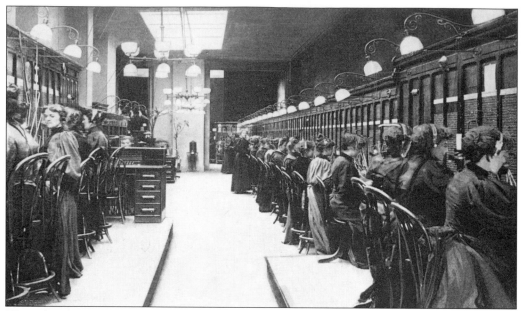

These female operators in the operating room of the New England Telephone and Telegraph Company connected the few thousand Bostonians who had telephones in the 1890s. Notice the numerous wires on the switchboard panels.

The American Bell Telephone Company was located in a handsome Romanesque building at 125 Milk Street. The company shared the building with the Western Union Company, the Postal Telegraph Cable Company, the Commercial Cable Company, the Direct United States Cable Company, and the New England Telephone Company.

Three

Downtown

This charming building was erected by Thomas Crease at the corner of Washington and School Streets in 1713. It became known as the Old Corner Bookstore in the early nineteenth century, when the bookstore shared the building with Ticknor and Fields, publishers, and a wood engraver. The Globe Corner Bookstore now calls this historical building home.

Tontine Crescent was designed by Charles Bulfinch and built on Franklin Street in 1795. The elegant crescent was built of brick but painted gray to simulate Portland Stone, and had a pavilion that connected the sixteen townhouses. The Boston Library Society was on the second floor and the Massachusetts Historical Society was on the third. The archway led to Summer Street and gave Arch Street its name.

Another of Bulfinch's magnificent achievements was the Cathedral of the Holy Cross, built on Franklin Street in 1803. The Roman Catholics of Boston had an impressive church adjacent to Tontine Crescent and fashionable Summer Street. In the background we can see the spire of Bulfinch's 1809 Federal Street Church.

The First Congregational Church was designed by Asher Benjamin and built on Chauncey Street in 1808. To the left is the Chauncey Hall School, a private preparatory school that later moved to the Back Bay.

The Welles-Gray duplex townhouse at the corner of Summer and Kingston Streets. Such fashionable townhouses were typical of the new form of housing introduced by Charles Bulfinch. Built of brick and painted to emulate stone, these houses boasted neo-classical details fashionable in Europe.

Bulfinch designed a granite octagonal church with an impressive portico and a superb spire for the New South Society in 1814. The church's location, at the junction of Bedford and Summer Streets, was known as Church Green for the now lost "green" (or lawn) in front of the church.

Daniel Webster's townhouse was opposite Church Green at the corner of Summer and High Streets. These townhouses, similar to the ones on Summer, High, Otis, Kingston, and Essex Streets, epitomize Boston architecture in the early nineteenth century.

The Boston Court House was designed by Bulfinch and built on School Street in 1810. It became Boston City Hall in 1822 and was used as such until the new City Hall, designed by Gridley J. Fox Bryant and Arthur Gilman, was built on the site in 1862.

The Old South Church was built in 1729 at the corner of Washington and Milk Streets. The brick additions on either side of the entrance were added in 1873 when a branch of the post office was relocated to this building.

The Old South Church, or "The Third Church of Boston," was organized in 1669. The "Mohawk Indians" who participated in the Boston Tea Party left from this site in 1775. By 1872, the congregation had already planned to move to the Back Bay and the structure became an historical museum.

The Brattle Square Church was designed by Thomas Dawes and built in 1772. It stood on Brattle Street, a street that is now buried under the Boston City Hall Plaza.

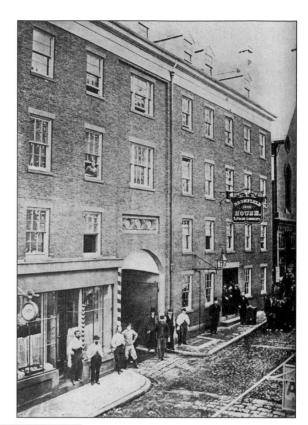

The Bromfield House was a hotel on Bromfield Street, opposite Province Street. The archway led to the hotel's stables. On the right is the Bromfield Street Methodist Church.

Prior to the Civil War the section of Washington Street south of Milk Street was lined with commercial enterprises, including printing and engraving shops, shoe shops, haberdasheries, and dry goods stores.

The section of Washington Street north of Water Street was known as "Cornhill." This area later became home to newspapers such as *The Boston Globe*, *The Herald Advertizer*, and *The Transcript*, and was known locally as "Newspaper Row."

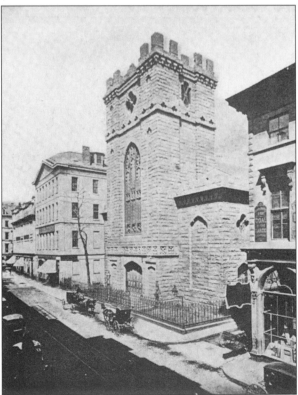

Trinity Church was located on Summer Street, on the site where Filene's is located today. Founded in 1733, this church was built by George Brimmer in the Boston "Gothick" style in 1829. It was destroyed by the Great Boston Fire of 1872.

This distinctive building, with its stepped gable end, faced City Hall at the corner of City Hall Avenue and School Street.

Boston City Hall was designed and built in 1862 by Gridley J. Fox Bryant and Arthur Gilman. With its projecting center, side wings, and modified mansard roof, it represents the finest example of French Second Empire architecture in Boston. The statue in the foreground is of Benjamin Franklin.

Looking north on Washington Street with Summer Street on the right. Horse-drawn omnibuses, such as the ones shown here, used to carry passengers through Boston's shopping districts. The spire of the Old South Church can be seen on the right.

The Macullar Parker Company, a "ready-made" clothing company, was located on Washington Street. This busy street scene shows Washington Street and Franklin Street (just to the left of the streetcar).

Jordan Marsh was founded by Eben Jordan in Boston in 1841, and its headquarters are still located at the corner of Washington and Summer Streets. At the turn of the century the store was comprised of two city blocks, making it Boston's largest department store.

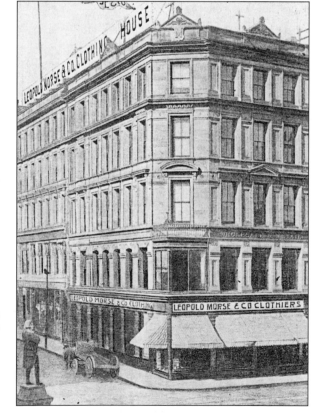

The Leopold Morse & Company was a clothing store located at the corner of Washington and Brattle Streets. Established in 1852, it sold to both wholesale and retail markets from an impressive building opposite Scollay Square.

"Newspaper Row," previously known as "Cornhill," was the section of Washington Street between Water and State Streets. Newspaper reporters used to crowd the streets here night and day.

This photograph shows a team from Manning & Son Safemovers hoisting an 8,000-pound Detroit safe up to an office at Oliver Ditson & Company. Using only simple pulley systems, these bonded truckdrivers lifted the safe up five stories with minimal effort.

The area where Summer and Bedford Streets meet was once a busy retail district. By 1875 office buildings had replaced earlier townhouses and a network of streetcars connected South Station to other parts of the city.

The corner of Franklin and Devonshire Streets used to be home to the elegant Tontine Crescent, but by the time this photograph was taken it was filled with skyscrapers housing banks and investment houses. The Old State House can be seen at the end of Devonshire Street.

The Boston Chamber of Commerce building was built between 1890 and 1892 by Shepley, Rutan, and Coolidge. This Romanesque Revival granite block structure has impressive windows, monumental arches, and a crenelated dormer roof line.

Congress Street was rebuilt with five-story buildings following the Great Boston Fire of 1872. This photograph shows the view looking towards Post Office Square.

The Boston Post Office was still in the early stages of its construction in 1872, which prevented the Great Fire from doing it much damage. The French Second Empire-style building stood between Milk Street (left) and Water Street and faced Post Office Square. The monument in the center of the square was designed by Peabody & Stearns. Erected in 1912, it was dedicated to the memory of George T. Angell, founder of the Massachusetts Society for the Prevention of Cruelty to Animals.

The New England Mutual Life Insurance Company was located on Milk Street between Pearl and Congress Streets. It also had its main entrance on Post Office Square.

The Boston Custom House was built in 1847. In 1915 a tower was added by Peabody & Stearns, making the building Boston's only skyscraper until the Hancock Tower on Boylston Street was built. In this photograph we can see the Board of Trade building on the left and on the Boston Chamber of Commerce building on the right.

The Boston Board of Trade building was built on India Street between State and Milk Streets in 1916. With its impressive arched entrance and limestone quoins, it is still an important part of the Waterfront. State Street can be seen on the right.

The Converse Building at the corner of Milk and Pearl Streets. Its red brick and limestone trim makes it stand out from the many office buildings in the area.

The Exchange Club, a
businessmen's club on
Milk Street, was
designed by Boston
architects Ball &
Dabney.

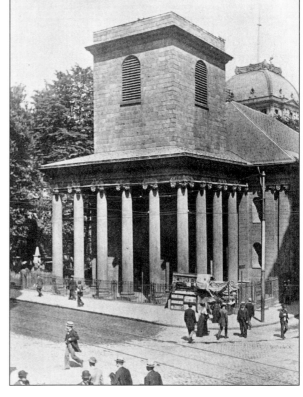

King's Chapel, at the corner of
Tremont and School Streets, was
designed by Peter Harrison. It was
built in 1750 and used as an Anglican
church until the Revolution, but in
1789 it became the first Unitarian
church in America. To the left is
King's Chapel Burying Ground, the
oldest cemetery in Boston and the
resting place for many of the founders
of Boston, including Governor John
Winthrop.

Four

Beacon Hill

Park Street leads to the Massachusetts State House, which was built between 1795 and 1798. The townhouses on the right of this photograph were designed by Charles Bulfinch and built in 1805 facing the Boston Common.

Doric Hall is a large public space with Doric columns that support the upper story of the Massachusetts State House. The statue on the left is of Governor John A. Andrew; the one in the center is of George Washington.

The Massachusetts State House was designed by Charles Bulfinch, Boston's premier architect, and built on Beacon Hill between 1795 and 1798. This turn-of-the-century photograph shows the rear wing that was added by Charles E. Brigham between 1889 and 1895. The wing was built of yellow brick to resemble the painted brick of the original building. The State House was painted a variety of colors in the nineteenth century.

42

This photograph shows the view looking down Park Street from the steps of the State House. On the left is the Amory-Ticknor House (which was designed by Bulfinch and built in 1804), the Union Club, the spire of the Park Street Church, and the Mall on the Boston Common.

The house at No. 2 Park Street (with the exterior shutters) was called the Warren House. The townhouses to the left of the Park Street Church were designed by Bulfinch and were used as residential dwellings until the early 1870s. Notice the recessed arcade on the first floor and the decorative cast iron balconies.

Park Street as seen from the Brewer Fountain on the Boston Common. Park Street was the quintessential Boston street—the combination of the rowhouses, trees, and fountains were reminiscent of early nineteenth-century London. On the right is the spire of Peter Banner's 1809 Park Street Church.

Tremont Street meets the Boston Common at its intersection with Park Street. The Common has been held in common trust for Bostonians since 1634. It was used for the grazing of cattle until 1830, when it was declared a park.

The drawing room of the Warren House contained a curious mixture of inherited family furniture and fashionable upholstered Victorian pieces. The Warrens had a large collection of paintings including an "imi-Titian," or a reproduction of Titian's *Cleopatra Dissolving the Pearl*, which can be seen to the left of the mantle. Many of the paintings were inherited by Rosamond Warren Gibson, and they are now on view at The Gibson House Museum in Boston's Back Bay.

In this view of the drawing room in the Warren House we can see between the doors a Victorian "etagere," or "what-not," displaying a wide variety of bibelots. With a patterned carpet, a gasolier with an extension to the center table's gas lamp, and a profusion of paintings and bronzes, this room is typical of the richly-decorated homes of Boston's "Brahmins" of this period.

This photograph, taken from the drawing room looking into the dining room, shows the large expandable dining table with its Klismo side chairs. The elaborately-carved door frames contained sliding doors that allowed the family to close off each room for privacy.

The Warrens' study was a semi-oval room with numerous bookcases to hold their vast library of books. The painting above the mantle is a portrait of Dr. Joseph Warren, a family ancestor who died during the Battle of Bunker Hill. His sword hangs above the painting.

The Hancock House stood near the State House on Beacon Hill. This famous house, constructed entirely of granite, was built in 1737 by Thomas Hancock, a wealthy Boston merchant. The house and the adjoining lands were inherited by John Hancock, a patriot of the Revolution and the first governor of Massachusetts. Though the house was a landmark even in its day, it was razed in 1863.

Jonathan Mason was one of the "Mount Vernon Proprietors" who purchased land belonging to John Singleton Copley on Beacon Hill, and had Charles Bulfinch lay out streets for development in 1795. Mason's house was built on Mount Vernon Street in 1802, and was a free-standing townhouse. Bulfinch had envisioned this new neighborhood with houses built on small lots rather than rowhouses, but only 45 Mount Vernon Street (built by Bulfinch in 1800) remains as it was originally built.

47

The Sears House was built on Beacon Street in 1819 facing the Boston Common. Designed by Alexander Parris and built of granite, this free-standing townhouse was enlarged with a second bay and a third story when it became the Somerset Club.

The twin mansions at 54 and 55 Beacon Street were designed by Asher Benjamin in 1807. With neo-classical details such as paired columns supporting a cast iron balcony, pilasters flanking swell bays, and a roof balustrade, these townhouses are impressive examples of Benjamin's skill as an architect.

Mount Vernon Street was lined with four-story townhouses that had created a unified appearance with a shared roof line. On the right is the Nichols House Museum, which was probably designed by Charles Bulfinch and built in 1804. The house has been preserved as an example of a Beacon Hill home and is open to the public.

Charles Street lies at the foot of Mount Vernon, one of the three hills of Boston (the other two are Beacon Hill and Pemberton Hill). Beacon Hill used to be much steeper—it was once as high as the State House dome—but it was cut down by the Mount Vernon Proprietors as part of their plans for the development of Mount Vernon. The land was carted down the hill and dumped, creating the "flat" of Beacon Hill west of Charles Street.

The Boston Athenaeum was founded in 1807 as a proprietary library. The "new" building at 10 1/2 Beacon Street was designed by Edward Clarke Cabot in 1846 and built between 1847 and 1849. It was then enlarged by Henry Forbes Bigelow in 1913. On the left of this photograph is the American Unitarian Society Headquarters; in the center is the house at the corner of Beacon and Somerset Streets where the Somerset Club was founded.

The "Reading Room" on the fifth floor of the Boston Athenaeum was added to the original building in 1913. The great arches and the barrel vault ceiling make quite an impression when one enters this room.

At the corner of Mount Vernon and Walnut Streets is a small house built of brick with one wall sheathed in wood planking. Though many of the townhouses on Beacon Hill are far grander, this 1802 house has a distinct charm.

The Somerset Club (formerly the Sears House) was enlarged in 1872. By this date, the open space street layout envisioned by Bulfinch for Beacon Street had been replaced by a unified streetscape created by the numerous townhouses built between 1830 and 1850.

The Massachusetts General Hospital was established in 1811 by Dr. John Collins Warren and Doctors Jackson, Gorham, Bigelow, and Channing. The first hospital building was designed by Charles Bulfinch and built in 1818 at the corner of Blossom and Allen Streets. The first use of ether in medicine took place in an 1847 operation performed in the great dome of this hospital.

This photograph shows a train crossing the Charles River Bridge between Boston and Cambridge at the turn of the century. Today the MBTA public transportation line known as the "Red Line" connects the Charles Street and Central stops.

The men of the Massachusetts 5th Regiment pass a reviewing stand on the steps of the State House as they depart for the Spanish-American War. On the left is the Shaw Memorial to Company 54, an African-American Civil War regiment led by Robert Gould Shaw. Dedicated in 1897, the memorial has a bas relief of Shaw with the soldiers by Augustus Saint Gaudens. The setting was designed by Charles McKim of McKim, Mead, and White.

The African Meeting House on Joy Street on Beacon Hill. In the early nineteenth century, Boston's African-American community lived on the western slope of Beacon Hill. The New England Anti-Slavery Society was formed at this church, and today it is a museum that preserves and teaches the history of its founders.

The altar and nave of the Church of the Advent are impressive examples of Victorian architecture. The screen which separated the altar from the nave was removed in this century but otherwise the church remains perfectly preserved.

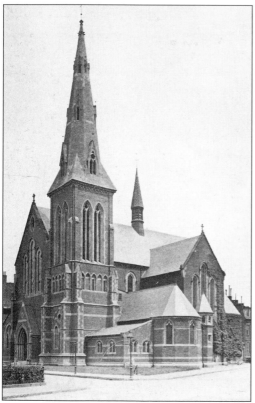

The Church of the Advent was founded in 1844, and the present church was designed by John H. Sturgis between 1879 and 1883. The church was built at the corner of Brimmer and Mount Vernon Streets on the "flat" of Beacon Hill.

Baseball was played on the Boston Common throughout the last century. This photograph, taken on July 4, 1913, shows a City Athletic Meet sponsored by the City of Boston. The event attracted a large audience, most of whom wore straw "boaters" to protect themselves from the sun.

Pemberton Square was once a residential square with rowhouses similar to those on Louisburg Square. The Suffolk County Court House (on the left) was built in 1889; shortly after it was erected, large office buildings dwarfed the remaining townhouses.

Westhill Place is a group of townhouses designed around a courtyard. Designed by Coolidge and Carlson in 1916, these townhouses had access to Storrow Drive (or the Charlesgate Bank as it was then known).

The steps from Brigham's addition to the State House led to Derne Street. This photograph shows a gentleman descending the staircase with Temple Street directly ahead.

Five

Tremont Street

Originally a residential neighborhood, Tremont Street began to see other developments even before the Civil War. This photograph shows King's Chapel (on the left), the Tremont Temple, the Park Street Church, and the Tremont House. The Tremont House (on the right with a projecting portico) was designed by Isaiah Rogers in 1828. Considered Boston's first luxury hotel, it survived until 1893, when an office building was built on its site.

Colonnade Row was built by Charles Bulfinch in 1810. The townhouses faced the Boston Common and extended from West Street to Mason Street.

Saint Paul's Church was built by Alexander Parris and Solomon Willard in 1820. With a colonnade and a massive pediment, its Greek Revival grandeur added much to Tremont Street. Today, it is the cathedral of the Episcopal Diocese of Massachusetts.

GRANARY BURIAL GROUND
OLD TREMONT HOUSE AND
TREMONT ST., IN 1880.

Tremont Street became a busy thoroughfare connecting Boylston Street and Scolly Square. On the left of this photograph is the Granary Burying Ground. This famous burial ground—Paul Revere, John Hancock, and Elizabeth Vergoose (or "Mother Goose," as she was better known) are buried here—was laid out in 1660 and named for the town granary that was located on the site of the Park Street Church.

The Boston Museum was built opposite the Granary Burying Ground on Tremont Street in 1841. It later became Gleason's Publishing Hall, where Frederick Gleason printed *Gleason's Pictoral Drawing Room Companion*. To the left of the museum is Tremont Temple, and on the far left the colonnade of King's Chapel can be seen.

The Park Street Church at the corner of Tremont and Park Streets was built by Peter Banner in 1809. This corner was known as "Brimstone Corner" for the fiery sermons delivered by the minister, but also because gunpowder was stored under the church during the War of 1812. The song "America" was first sung publicly in this church.

The Revere House was a well-known hotel designed by William Washburn in 1847. The hotel was basically an enlargement of the Boodt House, designed by Bulfinch and located at the corner of Cambridge and Bowdoin Streets. The Revere House was demolished by 1920, and the Saltonstall Building stands on its site.

Scollay Square was the area at the junction of Tremont, Cambridge, and Court Streets. It was named for an eighteenth-century Boston merchant, and was always a busy area; by the turn of this century it was a bustling section of the city with numerous stores and services. It was later home to the infamous "Old Howard" Theatre where Sally Keith and her "tassels" reigned.

The Boston Museum on Tremont Street (near Court Street) was designed by Hammatt Billings in 1846. Many famous actors and actresses of the nineteenth century performed in this "museum," so-called to enable proper Bostonians to attend the theatre under the pretense that they were broadening their minds rather than enjoying frivolous entertainment.

The Grand Foyer of the Boston Museum had a vaulted ceiling supported by monumental Corinthian columns. It also held historical exhibits, classical busts, and massive paintings depicting historical scenes that could be viewed during the intermission of the theatrical performances.

The Parker House was designed by Gridley J. Fox Bryant and built at the corner of Tremont and School Streets in 1854. It was an elegant hotel that served rolls that became so popular that "Parker House Rolls" are now available in every supermarket. To the right is a pediment of the Tremont Temple Baptist Church.

The lobby of the Parker House has marble columns, a marble reception desk, and portraits of the Parkers on either side of the doorway leading to the offices. The hotel's employees, from bellboys (shown here on the left) to chamber maids (on the right), worked to uphold the traditions of superb hotel accommodations and fine cuisine, which are still maintained to this day.

The dining room of the Parker House has large, arched windows that overlook School Street. An elegantly appointed room with classical details, huge potted palms, and electric chandeliers, it has always had a loyal following.

Houghton & Dutton was a department store located in former townhouses at the corner of Tremont and Beacon Streets. It supplied fine china, glassware, silver-plated goods, cloaks, undergarments, corsets, skirts, dry goods, and coffee. It survived until after World War II, when the buildings were demolished to build 1 Beacon Street.

Looking south down Tremont Street from the corner of Park Street. The Lafayette Mall was removed when the first underground subway system in the world was constructed between 1895 and 1897. The kiosks of the Park Street Station can be seen on the right, with Winter Street barely visible on the far left.

While the Park Street Church had not changed since its construction in 1809, by the time this photograph was taken around 1910 Park Street had become wholly commercial, as testified by the enormous billboard on the roof of the former Warren House.

Turn-of-the-century Bostonians must have marveled at the new and extremely modern underground subway system. Descending through clearly marked entrances, passengers would enter a noisy world of trolleys that could carry them swiftly to the other side of town.

The Park Street Subway Station was a tile-walled station with a ticket booth on the right and a platform on the left where one boarded the trolleys. This photograph shows two ladies awaiting the next trolley bound for Copley Square.

Tremont Street was a busy thoroughfare by 1910. On the left of this photograph is Winter Street, the cross street that connected Tremont and Washington Streets.

Masonic groups have been active in Boston since before the Revolution. This old Masonic Temple was built at the intersection of Tremont Street and Temple Place for the organization in 1831. The church-like building was used until 1858, when it was sold for use as a United States courthouse.

Tremont Street decked out for the 1913 Columbus Day Parade. The lively parade of marching bands, floats, and fraternities attracted thousands of Bostonians, as seen in this photograph of the activities near the corner of Tremont and Boylston Streets.

The Parkman Bandstand on the Boston Common. The bandstand, built to resemble a classical temple complete with Ionic columns, was built by the City of Boston. This photograph shows the United German Societies and Municipal Band presenting a concert in 1913.

Six
State and Court Streets

State Street, originally known as King Street, ran from the Old State House to Long Wharf. By the late nineteenth century it had become Boston's financial center and the earlier three-story buildings were quickly being replaced by multi-story office buildings. This photograph, taken in the middle of this period of change, shows the corner of Broad Street and the Old State House at the head of State Street.

The Declaration of Independence was first read to Bostonians from the balcony of the Old State House. Here, a Fourth of July celebration is enlivened by a re-enactment of the reading of the document by a costumed and bewigged orator.

The view looking east down State Street from the Old State House on a typical Flag day in the early 1920s. Many of the new office buildings sport American flags and the street is thronged with streetcars, carriages, and hacks. On the left is the site of 60 State Street; on the right is 53 State Street.

Cobb's Tea Room was at the corner of "Cornhill" and Court Street. The small shop was opened in 1883 and it offered a wide range of teas, including Earl Gray, Jasmine, India, Ceylon, China, and a variety of fine blends. A "tasting counter" allowed one to taste a freshly steeped cup of tea prior to making a purchase.

A view looking north on Washington Street from the intersection of Court Street (left) and State Street. Washington Street used to continue north, but today it ends with the plaza that leads to City Hall Plaza. The high-rise on the left is the Sears Building and the building towering over that is the Ames Building.

The Merchants Exchange was designed by Isaiah Rogers in 1841 and built on State Street (just east of Congress Street). Boston merchants would meet in this imposing Greek Revival building to discuss business and await word of their ships.

The section of State Street at the intersection with Commercial Street had a series of early nineteenth-century buildings housing shops, bars, taverns, and restaurants that served the needs of the local business community.

This view, looking west from the Stock Exchange on State Street, shows the Old State House in the foreground, the Ames Building on the right, and other Victorian office buildings in and around State, Court, and Washington Streets.

The Sears Building was built in 1868 at the corner of Washington and Court Streets. It was the first office building in Boston to have an elevator, a luxury deemed necessary because the building's seven floors would tire even those in the best of shape. Today, The Boston Company is located on its site.

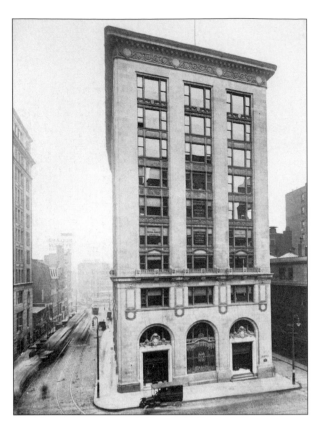

Merchants National Bank was located at 28 State Street, between Washington Street (left) and Congress Street. The high-rise office building that occupies the site today is the former home office of the Bank of New England.

The State Street Bank and Trust Company was located at 33 State Street, between Congress Street (left) and Quaker Lane. Today, the Bank of Greece occupies the first floor with professional offices above.

C.W. White & Company was located at 99 Court Street in a five-story building that included a factory where the company's trusses, elastic stockings, and lung protectors were made.

The Boston City Hall Annex was designed by Edward T.P. Graham and built on Court Street with Court Square forming a "U" around the building. This impressive building has monumental six-story Corinthian columns and caryatids above. Today, it is the headquarters of the Boston School Committee.

Looking east on Court Street with the Old State House in the distance. The Sears Block, a Greek Revival building, and numerous commercial concerns can be seen to the far left of the photograph.

Young's Hotel was at the corner of Court Street and Court Square. One of the many fashionable hotels in Boston in the 1890s, it had an important dining room and a private room where many clubs met for their annual dinners.

Seven

The South End

The City Hospital was designed by Gridley J. Fox Bryant and built between 1861 and 1864. The buildings that flanked the impressive domed hospital faced Worcester Square, and the whole complex, including the grounds, was bounded by Harrison Avenue and Concord, Albany, and Springfield Streets.

The Immaculate Conception Church was designed by Patrick J. Keeley and built on Harrison Avenue (between Concord and Newton Streets) in 1861. The church was staffed by the Jesuit Fathers and it is still a vital part of the South End. On the right is the original building of Boston College, which was founded by the Jesuits in 1863.

The nave and altar of the Immaculate Conception Church. The church had a monumental altar and a unique sounding board above the pulpit (on the left) to project the Jesuits' sermons.

The Boys' Latin and English High School on Warren Avenue was designed in 1887 by Boston City Architect George A. Clough. The school incorporated two distinct schools: the Latin School (founded in 1636) and English High School. Both schools continue to educate public schoolchildren, but on different sites.

The Cathedral of the Holy Cross was designed by Patrick C. Keeley, and was built between 1867 and 1875. It was located on Washington Street, between Malden Street (right) and Union Park Street, and was built of "Roxbury puddingstone," a material that was fashionable for church-building in the mid-nineteenth century.

The New England Conservatory of Music was located on Franklin Square at East Newton Street. Built in 1868, the French Second Empire-style building was originally designed by M.M. Ballou as the Saint James Hotel, and had over four hundred guest rooms. Today, the building is used for senior housing.

The Massachusetts Homeopathic Hospital was located on Harrison Avenue. Its numerous Victorian turreted buildings still survive and today constitute part of the Boston University Medical Center.

As Boston's population swelled, many of the open spaces became parks for the city's youth. One safe and easily-constructed winter attraction was the "coast." Here, children in the South End are enjoying one of these "substitute country hillsides."

The Home for Aged Men was designed by Gridley J. Fox Bryant on West Springfield Street in the South End. Intended as a hospital, the charming, ivy-clad building was used as a soldiers' home until 1869 when the Home for Aged Men (which was established in 1861) was opened. The Home for Aged Men, a retirement home for male senior citizens, was the last home of its architect.

The City of Boston Fire Department had its headquarters in an imposing yellow brick building that was constructed on the design of the Palazzo Vecchio in Florence, Italy. Today, this building is the Pine Street Inn, a refuge for Boston's homeless.

The repair shops of the city's fire department were located adjacent to the headquarters on Albany Street, just west of East Berkeley Street. Today this functional building is part of the Pine Street Inn.

Eight

The Great Boston Fire of 1872

The Great Boston Fire began in a hoop skirt factory at the corner of Summer and Kingston Streets. The evening of Saturday, November 9, 1872, was a quiet one, but the fire had a head start because the horses that normally pulled the fire engines were affected by an epizootic, and the fire spread beyond control before the replacement steam fire engines reached the scene. This photograph, taken just a few hours after the start of the fire, shows Winthrop Square falling victim to the flames.

When the fire reached the Old South Church, firemen tried to save the structure by placing wet blankets on the roof and playing water on its spire. Fierce patriotism and bravery saved "Old South" and stemmed the fire's spread.

The Merchant's Exchange was designed by Isaiah Rogers and built on State Street in 1841. A magnificent Greek Revival building, it was able to withstand the fire, thereby blocking the entry of the flames onto State Street. The exchange was demolished in 1891.

Summer Street, where the fire began, was burnt to the ground. This poignant photograph shows the crenelated spire of Trinity Church rising from the ruins. On the left, where the Jordan Marsh store stands today, are the smoldering ruins of C.F. Hovey & Company, R.H. Stearns & Company, and Shreve, Crump, & Low, all which were completely destroyed.

Summer Street had given way to commercialism by the time of the Civil War and it was totally devastated by the fire. Washington Street (near the corner of Milk Street and the Old South Church) fared better, due to its many four and five-story granite blocks. The fire seemed to stop at the carpet showroom of Foele, Torrey, & Company, but these buildings still had to be demolished.

This view, looking down Kingston Street from Summer Street, gives us an idea of the damage the fire did to this once elegant part of Boston.

Much of Boston had been built in such a haphazard manner that wood-framed colonial houses often stood side-by-side with more modern buildings. The lack of zoning, space, and varied building materials all added to the devastation of the Great Fire.

This view of Boston looking east on Summer Street from Washington Street has no real skyline: the fire, which burned for two days, destroyed over 40 acres of land and the entire area bounded by Boston Harbor and Washington, Summer, and Milk Streets. The streets were cleared within a few weeks and the long and costly process of rebuilding began in the spring of 1873.

"Cataract" Steamer No. 10 (from the firehouse at Mount Vernon Street) was photographed at Post Office Square after the fire had died. The half-completed post office can be seen in the background.

Nine

The Great Blizzard of 1888

The Great Blizzard of 1888 blanketed the city with a deep pile of snow. Through the snow-laden and ice-adorned trees of the Boston Common, we can just make out the State House. The storm was so severe and the snowfall so heavy that the trees look as if they are bowing to the capitol!

Park Street was practically inaccessible due to the deep snowdrifts caused by the winds blowing across the Common. On the far right is the Park Street Church and along Park Street Bulfinch's townhouses lead up to Beacon Street.

Snowplowing was unheard of a century ago, when the wisdom of the day decreed that rolling the snow was the most efficient way to make the streets accessible. This photograph shows Beacon Street after it had been rolled by "pungs" so the horse-drawn sleighs could glide along the packed snow, their bells ringing in the sharp wind. Walnut Street is on the right. The house with the projecting chimney was the home of John Phillips, who became the first mayor of Boston in 1822.

The Back Bay ablaze with bright white snow, as seen in a wonderful photograph taken from the roof of a townhouse on Walnut Street. The roofs in the foreground are those of the townhouses along Chestnut Street, looking towards Charles Street. The spires of the Back Bay churches are, from left to right, Arlington Street Church, Trinity Church, Central Congregational Church (now the Church of the Covenant), New Old South Church, the First Baptist Church, and the Church of the Advent.

A veritable winter wonderland: Beacon Street, near Walnut Street, just after the Great Blizzard of 1888. The townhouse on the right is 40 Beacon Street, which would later become the Women's City Club. The house two doors to the left (with the double bay facade) is the Somerset Club. With snow banked on fences, steps, and sidewalks, this New England storm was one that would be remembered for decades.

Ten

Boylston Street and Park Square

The new Park Square
Station was built by
Peabody & Stearns in
1872 as the depot of the
New York, New Haven,
& Hartford Railroad. An
impressive Victorian
railroad station, Park
Square had also been
embellished with a statue
of Abraham Lincoln at
the time of the
Emancipation
Proclamation of 1863.

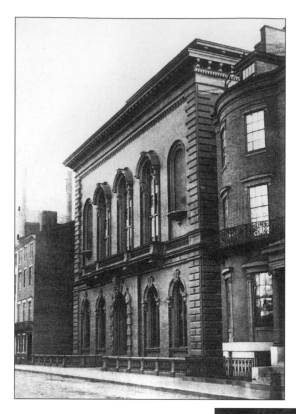

The Boston Public Library was designed by Charles K. Kirby and dedicated on January 1, 1858. Located on Boylston Street just west of Tremont Street, the beautiful Romanesque Revival building had soaring arched windows and quoining on the corners of the building and around the entrance. The building was razed in 1899, and the Colonial Theatre was built on its site.

Bates Hall was an impressive reading room in the Boston Public Library. With a vaulted ceiling that rose three stories, free-standing Corinthian columns, and a library collection that has become one of the finest in the world, this library was one of the reasons that Boston was known as the "Athens of America" in the Victorian era.

The Winthrop House was a hotel at the corner of Tremont and Boylston Streets. It was purchased by the Grand Lodge of Masons in 1859 and used as their lodge until 1864, when the upper stories were destroyed by fire.

The new Masonic Temple that was built after the fire was an impressive Gothic Revival building designed by Merrill Wheelock in 1867. The building had rooms for the lodge as well as businesses (including a furniture store and a savings bank) on the first floor.

This elegant building, the third Masonic Temple to be built at the corner of Tremont and Boylston Streets, was completed in 1899. At the turn of the century it was the headquarters for the Grand Lodge of Massachusetts and for thirteen Blue Lodges. It also had retail space on the first floor.

The Steinert Hall Building, with its two-story arched windows and elegant cornice, still stands opposite the Boston Common at the corner of Boylston and Carver Streets.

The showrooms of the Steinert & Sons Company offered upright pianos, baby grands, grands, and concert grands to Bostonians. After agreeing to purchase one of the many different pianos, one would deal with the cashier behind the grill on the right.

The lobby of the Hotel Touraine was a marble-encased room. With a grand staircase, potted plants, and marble columns supporting a richly-coffered ceiling, this fashionable residential and transient hotel was a favorite in Boston.

The Hotel Touraine still stands at the corner of Boylston and Tremont Streets. It is a ten-story building with a fine view of the Boston Common. Today it is an apartment building with retail space facing Tremont Street on the first floor.

The German Room was one of the three dining rooms in the Hotel Touraine. It was not as formal or elegant as the main dining room, but it did have Tutonic columns and a fireplace and chandeliers similar to those produced in Germany. The trophies around the room incorporate animal heads and crossed swords.

Architectural firms Blackall, Clapp, & Whittemore and Little & Russell worked together to design the Little Building. It faces the Boston Common at the corner of Boylston and Tremont Streets.

The arcaded shopping area of the Little Building meant that office employees could shop in comfort, even in bad weather. Of course, they always kept a sharp eye on the clock so they wouldn't return to their office late.

The Frog Pond on the Boston Common is an attractive place during the summer months. This late nineteenth-century photograph was taken from Beacon Street and it shows the ornate benches and fountains that were on the Common at that time.

This Victorian couple has paused in their perambulation around the Public Garden to admire the fountains and grounds. On the left is the greenhouse where many of the plants for the flower beds were cared for during the winter months.

Eleven

The Back Bay

The swan boats in the Public Garden are what most people picture when they think of Boston. They were inspired by the opera *Lohengren* which was a favorite of the Pagets, the family responsible for introducing the swans to the "Lagoon." The townhouses on Arlington Street (left) and Beacon Street can be seen in the distance.

The Public Garden was laid out on land "reclaimed" from the marshes of Back Bay. By 1850, the marshes bounded by what would become Charles, Beacon, Arlington, and Boylston Streets had been filled in and was laid out with serpentine paths, formal gardens, and playing fountains. This *c.* 1875 photograph shows the equestrian statue of President George Washington that had been sculpted by Robert Ball and erected in the Public Garden in 1872.

The Ether Monument was erected in the Public Garden to commemorate the first use of ether in an operation at the Massachusetts General Hospital in 1847.

The *Maid of the Mist* was a popular statue in the Public Garden.

This view, taken looking west in the Public Garden, shows the suspension bridge lit by the beautiful yet eerie light of gas lanterns. The uniform rooflines of the townhouses on Commonwealth Avenue can be seen in the distance.

In the romantic late Victorian era, the swan boats had brightly-striped awnings to protect their passengers from the sun. In this photograph, the boats are passing under the suspension bridge. The well-loved bridge was designed by William Gibbons Preston, and it is the smallest suspension bridge in the world.

Many generations of Boston's youth have enjoyed riding on the swan boats, whether for a lark with friends or for a romantic heart-to-heart with a suitor. The summertime ritual of waiting on the wood dock for a ride and gliding on the pond still enchants young and old alike. On the right of this picture one can also see the tower of the Park Square Station.

104

The Public Garden had been laid out in 1837, but it wasn't until the 1850s that the Back Bay was filled in with soil brought from Needham, Massachusetts. In the foreground is the corner of Charles and Beacon Streets and on the far left are the trees on Arlington Street.

This photograph, taken from the dome of the Massachusetts State House, shows how vastly different the Back Bay looked in 1850, when it consisted almost entirely of unusable marshland. Beacon Street was laid out in 1814 as the "Mill Dam" connecting Boston and Brookline, but problems with this solution arose when the lack of tidal flow along the Charles River meant that the water remained stagnant, causing noxious odors for Boston residents.

The Arlington Street Church was designed by Arthur Gilman and built in 1859 at the corner of Arlington and Boylston Streets. It was originally known as the Federal Street Church, as the congregation had moved from Federal Street to the Back Bay. Their church was the first to be built on the "new" land of the Back Bay.

The spire of the Arlington Street Church has always been a significant landmark in Boston. This photograph was taken looking across the Public Garden; it shows Newbury Street on the right, and on the far right three townhouses that were designed by Richard Morris Hunt and then demolished in 1928 to make way for the Ritz Carlton Hotel.

By the time this photograph was taken in 1895, the Back Bay was almost completed. On the far left is the open land of the Boston Common, with the Public Garden beyond. On the right is Beacon Street, which runs from Beacon Hill through Brookline and was laid out with many fashionable townhouses.

Catherine Hammond Gibson (the widow of Boston sugar merchant John Gardiner Gibson) and her nephew Samuel Hammond Russell contracted Edward Clarke Cabot to design adjoining townhouses at 135 and 137 Beacon Street. Built in 1859, the houses were among the first townhouses in the Back Bay, and now 137 Beacon Street is The Gibson House Museum, Boston's only Victorian house museum and the most important and impressive historic house in the Back Bay.

The Natural History Museum was designed by William Gibbons Preston and built in 1863 on Berkeley Street between Boylston and Newbury Streets. Filled with stuffed animals, dinosaur eggs, and other curiosities, the museum provided hours of education and entertainment until 1947, when it was moved to Cambridge to become the Museum of Science.

This view of Berkeley Street looking south from Beacon Street shows that residential and ecclesiastical buildings harmonized comfortably. On the right is the First Church which was designed and built by Ware and van Brundt between 1865 and 1868. In the distance is the spire of the Central Congregational Church, now the Church of the Covenant.

Marlborough Street, named for the British duke, was laid out as a cross street. The townhouses on this street were less grand than those on Beacon Street and Commonwealth Avenue, and consequently they were always easier to staff. Though all townhouses required staff such as butlers, maids, and cooks, these smaller houses were more manageable. Today Marlborough Street is an elegant tree-lined street.

Charles Hammond Gibson Jr. was the third generation of the Gibson family to live at 137 Beacon Street. He graduated from Saint Paul's and went on to study at the Massachusetts Institute of Technology' s School of Architecture for a year, prior to traveling through England and France. In the late 1930s he established his family's townhouse as the Gibson House Museum. The museum preserves three generations of his family's history and is also one of the most remarkably preserved houses in Boston.

The Massachusetts Institute of Technology (MIT) was incorporated in 1861. This photograph shows the Rogers Building, MIT's first building, which was built on Boylston Street in 1867. It was named for William Barton Rogers, the first president of the college, and designed by William Gibbons Preston. The building was razed in 1937 and "The New England," the home of a life insurance company, was built on its site.

The Young Men's Christian Association (YMCA) was a fanciful step-gabled building designed by Sturgis & Brigham and built in 1883 at the corner of Boylston and Berkeley Streets.

The MIT School of Applied Mechanics (the Engineering Building) was built next to the Rogers Building at the corner of Boylston and Clarendon Streets.

MIT students studied "the efficiency of screw-jacks" and other useful subjects in the laboratories at the world-renowned college.

The Hotel Vendome was Boston's largest hotel in the 1890s. The first portion, at the corner of Dartmouth Street and Commonwealth Avenue, was designed by William Gibbons Preston in 1871. An enormous addition was added by J.F. Ober in 1881. Following a disastrous fire in 1972, the building was remodeled into affordable condominiums in the Back Bay.

This 1900 view, taken from the Hotel Vendome looking west along Commonwealth Avenue, shows the grandest street in Massachusetts nearing completion. With a green space in the center, "The Mall" led to the Public Garden.

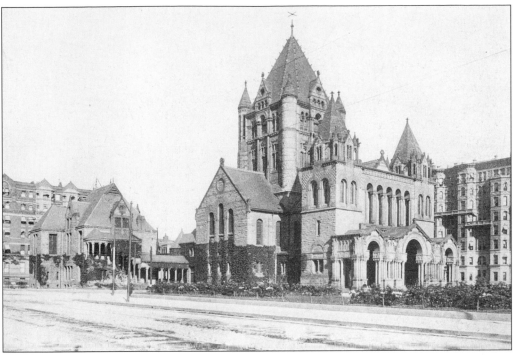

The congregation of Trinity Church moved to the Back Bay after the Great Boston Fire of 1872 destroyed its church on Summer Street. Designed by Henry Hobson Richardson and consecrated in 1877, this Romanesque masterpiece still dominates Copley Square.

Henry Hobson Richardson (1838–1886) as an undergraduate at Harvard. One commentator on his style of architecture said after his untimely death that his works were the "outpourings of a copious, direct, large, and simple mind."

The Boston Museum of Fine Arts was incorporated in 1870 and the original building was designed by Sturgis and Brigham in 1876. An addition doubled the size of the museum in 1890. Despite its plethora of rich details, such as tablets depicting the "Genius of Art" and "Art and Industry," the Gothic Revival building was razed in 1911 to make way for the Copley Plaza Hotel.

This photograph of art students posing in a gallery in the Museum of Fine Arts shows many of the paintings that still grace the walls of the new Huntington Avenue building.

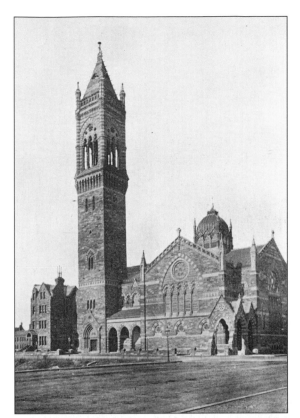

The new Old South Church was designed by Cummings & Sears and built in 1875 at the corner of Boylston and Dartmouth Streets. The congregation had moved from the Old South Meetinghouse to this "new" church, thus the name. Notice the parsonage on the left and the open space beyond.

The 3,285-pound bell of the new Old South Church was raised 190 feet up to the Venetian bell tower by the employees of the Bowen Safe and Machinery Mover and General Teamster company.

The Central Congregational Church was designed by Richard M. Upjohn and built at the corner of Berkeley and Newbury Streets in 1867. The architect used Roxbury "puddingstone" to create this Gothic building. The stone was quarried locally and made famous in Holmes' poem *The Dorchester Giant.* Today this is the Church of the Covenant.

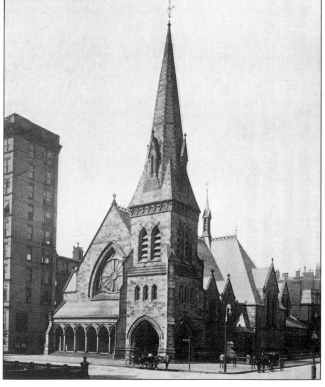

The First Church was designed by Ware & van Brunt and built in 1868. A beautiful stone church, it had a disastrous fire in the late 1960s and was rebuilt with the existing walls but a modern interior. Today it serves a Unitarian congregation and it is known as the First and Second Church in Boston.

The Boston Public Library was designed by McKim, Mead, and White and built facing Copley Square on Dartmouth Street in 1895. Once the original library building was outgrown by both collections and customers, the trustees decided to build a library in the Back Bay where "sculpture and painting (could) join hands with architecture, as they never have in modern times." The building was designed to emulate an Italian palazzo, and it covered over 1 1/2 acres of land. The trolley on the right is traveling along Boylston Street, carrying passengers from Brighton to the downtown shops and businesses.

Trinity Church (left) is a grand church that once fronted onto Huntington Avenue, which can be seen in front of the portico. On the right is the 1912 Copley Plaza Hotel.

The First Baptist Church was designed by H.H. Richardson and built at the corner of Clarendon Street and Commonwealth Avenue in 1871. It was originally built for the Brattle Square Church, but it later became the First Baptist Church, or "the Church of the Holy Beanblowers." This nickname is a reference to the life-sized angels with trumpets which resemble beanblowers.

The Venetian Room in the Hotel Brunswick was a luxurious parlor with a Venetian glass chandelier and richly-upholstered furniture. With paintings in large, carved, gold-leafed frames—and a frieze of Iris—this room really is the epitome of the decorating and furnishing styles of the day.

The Hotel Brunswick was built at the corner of Boylston and Berkeley Streets. With its rotunda and fashionable Victorian decorations, it was another popular hotel in Boston.

The Hotel Victoria was built at the corner of Dartmouth and Newbury Streets. A fashionable residential hotel, it had a fine dining room and an unique exterior, especially the crenelated cornice.

As development in Boston continued to move the heart of the city west, residents began to choose apartment houses rather than private townhouses. The Hotel Puritan is located at 390 Commonwealth Avenue, and it offered patrons rooms to rent for easy living without the cost of upkeep.

The Harvard Club of Boston is on Commonwealth Avenue, just west of Massachusetts Avenue, and it faces the statue of Leif Eriksson on "The Mall."

The Boston Athletic Association was located at the corner of Exeter and Blagden Streets. The patterned-brick clubhouse had a boathouse on the Charles River and a gun club in West Newton in addition to these clubrooms.

This photograph, taken looking west from the Hotel Somerset, shows us the fashionable townhouses that lined Commonwealth Avenue. In the distance is Kernmore Square, known prior to 1930 as Governor's Square. The area in the distance would later become the campus of Boston University.

The Church of Christ, Scientist, was founded by Mary Baker Eddy in 1879. Its "mother church," the First Church of Christ, Scientist, was erected between 1894 and 1906 on land between Massachusetts and Huntington Avenues and Falmouth, Norway, and Saint Paul Streets. In the late 1970s a portico was added to the facade of the vast, domed edifice by the architect I.M. Pei.

The Romanesque Revival stone church was adjacent to the residential development taking place near Massachusetts Avenue.

The Charles River Esplanade was a park that abutted the rear of the Back Bay townhouses on Beacon Street. Through the generosity of Mrs. James Jackson Storrow, the park was laid out with trees, and enough space for concerts such as those held today at the "Hatch Shell," a large concert pavilion.

The Hotel Kenmore was built on Commonwealth Avenue. It later became Chamberlayne Junior College before being converted to condominiums.

Twelve
The Fenway

The Fenway separates Boston and Brookline. It was originally known as the "Muddy River," but at the turn of this century Olmstead Associates—the group responsible for the "Emerald Necklace," a plan which envisioned green space surrounding the city—created the Fenway that we know today just west of the Back Bay. The Fenway saw very little residential development, but rather became an area of hospitals, schools, museums, and institutions.

One Back Bay resident who did build a residence in the Fenway was Isabella Stewart Gardner, whose "Venetian Palace" at the corner of the Fenway and Worthington Street (seen here on the left) was dedicated on New Year's Day in 1903. The noted museum was conceived by its founder as the Isabella Stewart Gardner Museum many years before it was built. On the right is Simmons College, a women's college that was chartered in 1899 to "enable its pupils to acquire an independent livelihood." Named for John Simmons, a Boston merchant, it is still providing higher education in the Fenway.

Children's Hospital was built on Longwood Avenue at the corner of Blackfan Street. An impressive domed building with four Corinthian columns supporting a portico, it provided health care for the youth of Boston. Today, though Children's Hospital has increased many times in size, the original building echoes an earlier time.

The Second Church in Boston built their classical church in 1913 on Audubon Circle, near Brookline. The congregation had been founded at the North End and later moved to Boylston Street in the Back Bay. When the congregation joined the First Church of Boston, becoming the First and Second Church, this building was sold to the Ruggles Baptist Church.

The Wentworth Institute was founded in 1904 to provide a mechanical and technical education for young men. The large school was built on Ruggles Street between Huntington Avenue and Parker Street. Seen here, the Wentworth baseball team posed in 1924 in front of the school.

The Fenway attracted the Massachusetts Horticultural Society, which had been founded in 1829. Designed by Wheelwright & Haven and built in 1900 at the corner of Massachusetts and Huntington Avenues, this impressive French Academic building served as the headquarters of the society for many years. Today, the interior houses numerous professional and institutional offices.

Symphony Hall was designed by McKim, Mead, and White and built in 1900 at the corner of Massachusetts and Huntington Avenues.